HOW TO GROW YOUR
BUSINESS USING INSTAGRAM

HOW TO GROW YOUR BUSINESS USING INSTAGRAM

THE ULTIMATE GUIDE
FOR BADASS BUSINESS OWNERS
AND MARKETERS LOOKING TO GENERATE
TRAFFIC, LEADS, AND SALES
USING INSTAGRAM

AMEL KILIC

"The road to success and the road to failure are almost exactly the same."

– Colin R. Davis

Contents

Introduction

Let's Clear Something Up

Big butts and food...

I don't know why, but many business owners think that is Instagram's only asset. Now, I do acknowledge that there are a lot of accounts on Instagram that are not monetizable, but then again, who doesn't like nice butts and food! *We will not go there now;* I just want you to understand that there is a lot of consumer attention on the app. Instagram is soon to hit over 1 billion users. *Are you going to tell me that your target audience is not on Instagram?* There are almost over 200 million active users daily; our goal is to turn this consumer attention into loyal paying customers for our businesses and clients.

I understand that many people are resistant to almost everything that is new—I get it—it is a survival mechanism. The issue here is that if you do not adapt to changes, your business will fail. Just take a look at how many big corporations filed bankruptcy in the last few years. It was mainly because they did not adapt to market changes. Companies that are one-hundredth of their size are the ones running them out of business. How is this even possible? The answer: these companies understood where their customers are and how to gain their trust—at a low cost.

I want you to think about this...

Two college students decided that they wanted to create stylish and inexpensive watches. They received some crowdfunding and dropped out of college. Understanding who their market was, they decided to start using Instagram to promote their products. Just like any Instagram user, they created an account and started posting content. However, they understood the power of influencers, so they hired Instagram influencers to display images of the watches on their personal account. Fast forward a year later, they generated one million dollars in sales by using Instagram alone. The next year, they generated $7 million. If you are a millennial or a watch fanatic, you have probably heard of the company; it is MVMT.

Now, let me be honest...

You are probably less likely to be capable of scaling at that pace. What allowed MVMT to scale so fast and become successful was that they were building a brand around their product. We will talk about branding later on in the book. Another critical factor was that there were not that many competitors on Instagram five years ago. It is a little tougher to gain consumer attention now. There are over 25 million business accounts on Instagram. A little over 70% of all businesses are already on Instagram. The good news is that many of them do not understand how to fully optimize their account in order to generate traffic and sales—but you will, after reading this book and implementing the strategies that we will cover.

The reason most businesses do not have an optimized Instagram account is that it is not that simple. A lot of fundamental effort goes into setting up your account correctly and staying consistent with it. The good thing is that after the hard work is completed, all you have to do in order to continue growing your Instagram account and business is to stay consistent. Only through consistent activity and invested time will you notice the ultimate power of Instagram marketing and the power of using it to build your business.

Another good thing about Instagram is that no matter what industry your business is in, you can use Instagram to scale it. I hear remarks like, "My clientele is not on Instagram" or "My business is different; it will not work for us," way too often. Please take a second right now and do yourself and me a favor. Take that opinion, write it down on a piece of paper, and burn it! No matter if you are a small family-owned cupcake store, a lawyer, doctor, or Google, everyone wants either more awareness, sales, credibility, or loyalty, which you can obtain with Instagram. Your business goals are only an optimized Instagram away!

Instagram is continuously releasing business-focused features. They are literally working in your favor if you are a business owner or marketer. I mean, why would they not? The more value they can bring businesses, the more money the business will spend on ads and monetization.

I want to share one more story before we jump into the Instagram strategies to grow your business. Since most people have dogs, I will use them for this example. Say you were looking for a new dog groomer and you happen to be following a mobile dog groomer on Instagram who consistently posts before and after images of their work. They also display images of the team and their business, and maybe they even engaged with you previously on Instagram. On the flip side, there is another dog groomer's Instagram account which has a few old and low-quality images. They have a static URL and just a phone number in their bio. Who would you choose to take your dog to? Hope you see the importance of having a high quality, optimized Instagram account.

More and more people are looking up businesses on Instagram before using their service. Instagram is a qualifier; I don't want you losing business because you do not have an Instagram account that is set up to convert.

If you don't believe me, think about a time when an associate recommended a particular restaurant, realtor, or even a clothing brand. Did you look them up on Instagram to verify their credibility? I know that I do it all the time, and more users will also do so as Instagram continues to grow.

As you can probably already tell, this book is not going to be your regular cookie-cutter book of tips on how to grow your Instagram. This book is created for badass business owners and marketers who are looking to learn the raw truth on how to optimize and monetize Instagram accounts to grow your or your clients business and brand. I will give you all the top strategies to help grow your Instagram account the correct way so that you can start generating awareness, leads, and sales.

Just for credibility purposes, we run one of the top Instagram growth and optimization services in Florida. What sets us apart from other marketing companies is our focus. Most marketing companies focus on growing your Instagram account; we focus on growing your business using Instagram. I hope you can see the difference, and if you do not, you are in trouble. There is no benefit of growing your Instagram with followers that you cannot convert into paying customers. Understanding the different approaches will define your success with Instagram.

"If you are not willing to risk the usual, you will have to settle for the ordinary."

– Jim Rohn

Chapter 1

Define Your Goal

What is your goal with Instagram?

This is an excellent and essential question—you better know what your goal is with Instagram. We all understand the importance of setting up goals; goals with Instagram are no different. You are more likely to succeed in growing your business if you have specific goals set. Your Instagram goal can be to build trust, awareness, credibility, or revenue, for example. It may even be a few of those in conjunction, but make sure that you have a defined goal. The reason I want you to identify your goal before we start setting up your Instagram account is that as you start implementing the strategies, each strategy will be primed to your Instagram goal. If the entire Instagram account is not in sync with your goal and is not optimized to meet your objective, your account will not convert, and you will not see any results.

This initial step is what will separate you from your competitors on Instagram. So that you understand how detailed your goal needs to be, I will give you an oversight of a marketing consultation that I conduct with clients.

The conversation would be very similar to the example below. By the way, I'm not as big of an asshole as I will make myself sound. I just want you to get the idea of how targeted your goal needs to be.

Business owner

"Hey, I noticed your Instagram account and I wanted to grow my account as well."

Instagram Expert

"Hey, thanks for reaching out to me. I would love to help you grow your account. If you don't mind me asking, what is your goal with Instagram?"

Business Owner

"I just want more followers and engagement."

Instagram Expert

"Okay, so if I was able to help you bring in more engagement and followers from users in Germany, would you be satisfied? "

Business Owner

"No, I need followers that live in Tampa."

Instagram Expert

"Oh, okay! Now, I do understand that your business sells high-end suits. If I was able to grow your Instagram with followers who are teenagers with a passion for basketball, located in Tampa, would you find value in that?"

Business Owner

"No, I want to target businessman and entrepreneurs in Tampa."

Instagram Expert

"Ah, now we are getting somewhere! Now let us dive deeper into your Instagram goal."

The next questions are:

- What are their hobbies

- Who are your competitors on Instagram

- What part of town are they located in, and

- Where do they usually hang out

In the space provided below, write down your Instagram goal and remember to be specific.

_____

_____

_____

_____.

Great job, you are already ahead of 80% of Instagram users looking to grow their business using the platform. If you did not write down your goal, I want you to go back and do it. It is a crucial step, and I will explain why.

The Instagram platform consists of many different channels and variables. If you do not have an unambiguous goal, your business message will get lost. When it comes to fully optimizing your Instagram account, every single aspect of the platform needs to be in sync with your goal. Your Instagram story, feed, comments, and bio all need to be correlated to your specific goal. When you are implementing an action on Instagram, ask yourself if the action is going to help you attain your goal. If the answer is no, redo it!

Okay, let us jump back into our conversation with the business owner, who at least now knows who his target audience is.

Business Owner:
"They typically go to coffee shops such as Oxford Exchange and Buddy Brew, and my competitor is the Suit Supply Store."

Instagram Expert:
"Perfect! Now we know where to find them. If they go to those places, there is a big chance that they are following those accounts on Instagram (I'll explain how this helps later in the book). Now, I know that you mentioned that you want to grow your Instagram following and engagement, but what are you looking to get out of that?"

Business Owner:
"Well, I am trying to grow my awareness and sales."

After a few questions, the business owner has figured out his specific goal with Instagram. His goal is to increase sales by targeting entrepreneurs and businessman in Tampa who go to Oxford Exchange and Buddy Brew and who are presumably buying their suits at the Suit Supply store.

Before we move forward, I want you to rewrite your Instagram goal as I just did for the business owner above. Include as much detail about your potential client as you can. You need to understand your customers in order to target them and convert them into a sale.

_____

_____

_____

_____

_____.

When setting up your business goals, it is vital to set goals that motivate you. Just like money, it is the value they bring that motivates us to chase it. Your goal needs to have a higher value than a few meaningless words that you just wrote above. There is a high chance of giving up on your goal if it does not serve a higher purpose. As I mentioned earlier, growing your business on Instagram will not be easy. The reason most users quit is that their purpose was not stronger than their desire to quit.

I actually have an excellent tip to help you define the value in your goal. Remember when you were younger, and you had to explain to your parents why you wanted to do something, or nowadays, when you want to convince your friends on why your goal is worthwhile? Well, I want you to do the same now. Imagine that you have a goal and you are trying to convince your parents or friends to believe in it. What would you tell them?

Go ahead and write down the value that your goal will bring you and others.

_____

_____

_____

_____

_____.

As you start optimizing your Instagram account, you will be referencing back to your goal, making sure that everything you implement on your account will help you reach your Instagram goal. Continue asking yourself, will this help me achieve my goal?

"People who succeed have momentum. The more they succeed, the more they want to succeed, and the more they find a way to succeed. Similarly, when someone is failing, the tendency is to get on a downward spiral that can even become a self-fulfilling prophecy."

— Tony Robbins

Chapter 2

Learn From Your Competitors

Mastering Instagram Skills

Considering that you are reading this book, you are presumably not monetizing your Instagram account just yet. However, you have competitors that are! I have an extensive business tip that I would like to share with you right now. If you are looking to master your Instagram skills, why not learn from your competitors. They already understand how to grow and monetize their Instagram account, which is allowing them to grow their business.

The biggest obstacle in this strategy is your ego. No one likes to accept the fact that their competitors are better than they are, but you have to face the truth here. Your competitors are better than you when it comes to monetizing their Instagram account—but don't worry, they are probably only monetizing it on a small scale. You will take some tips from them and mold it with the tips I will give you in this book, and you will crush them. Before you know it, they will be learning from you.

After you find your competitors on Instagram, I want you to take a look at their bio, content, captions, stories, call to actions, links, and posting frequency. We will start optimizing all of this on your Instagram account in the next chapter, but I want you to figure out what is working for your competitors.

Bio

We are going to start with your competitor's bio. A bio can be lengthy and descriptive or short and precise. The preference for the bio is very subjective, but you should take a look at your competitor's bio and notice what all of them have in common.

- Are their bios divided with each key point on its own line, or is it all in one paragraph?
- Is there a call to action in the bio?
- Is the URL link leading us to their homepage or a landing page?

- Does it seem as they have a funnel when you click on their URL link?

The reason you need to know this data is that your potential clients are responding to your competitors Instagram strategy and sales methods. It is essential to understand what is working for them so that you can mold it to your strategy.

Now, take a look at their content.

- Is their content customer-oriented, or is it primarily focused on the staff and their product?
- What is the quality of their content?
- Do they have a theme?
- What is the posting ratio between personal and businesses content?

You may ask me, "Why do I need to know all of this?" Let me reiterate once again; your competitors are already accomplishing what you are looking to accomplish with Instagram. They are a step ahead of you. Having this data is essential to understanding their strengths and their weaknesses. You cannot beat them unless you understand their tactics.

In addition to that, another reason I want you to be aware of your competitors is because every business's Instagram marketing strategy is going to be slightly different. What may work for one business may not work so well for another business. There is not an ultimate marketing guide that would work for every business owner. I will explain why in the example below.

A "cupcake" business that is looking to generate more awareness and sales will do very well with content that is friendly and family-oriented. They would post content of kids coming into the store, the process of making the cupcakes, and their involvement in the community. On the other hand, if a construction company decided to utilize Instagram to grow their business, they will do well with images of their projects, the team behind the projects, and their project guarantees. Understanding what content works well for your competitors will give you a better idea on the content that you should be focused on when you start posting.

While we are looking at their content, take a look at their captions. If you are not sure what a caption is, it is the text beneath the images. The caption plays a big part in optimizing your Instagram account to convert followers into paying customers.

Do your competitor's caption consist of a story or is it concise and bold?

- Are they tagging anyone in their caption?
- Do they have a call to action?

By now you will have a good idea on what type of content and captions your competitors are utilizing. The next step will be more analytical. Take a look at the engagement on their posts. After you find their most engaging content, figure out what they did differently compared to their other posts. Having this information will allow you to focus on providing the content that your audience is more likely to engage with and be intrigued by.

How Frequently Should I Post?

The next analytical step will answer the inquiries every novice Instagram users perpetually asks. How frequently do I need to post? I will give you our own verified tips later in the book, but right now, I want you to focus on your competitors. When you start looking at their content, look for the date on the posts. Take notice of the frequency of their posts. Again, the cupcake store can get away with posting three pictures a day while the construction company will probably only post about once a day.

- Are the posts a day apart or a few days apart?
- How often do they post multiple images in a single day?

Call To Action

The last thing that you should take a look at is your competitors call to actions. Call to actions are very important in converting followers to paying customers. Take a look at your competitor's bio, images, stories, and captions. Do they have any call to actions, and if they do, what are they announcing? Are they soft selling or hard selling? If you found a successful Instagram account, you will find plenty of call to actions throughout their bio, captions, and stories.

Understanding your competitors is just as important as understanding your customers. Being aware of what they are doing will allow you to position your business as a leader in your industry, allowing you to attract your potential clients over them. I know that this chapter had a lot of work, and it may take some time until you collect all of that information, but do not skip it. Knowing what your competitors have implemented will allow you to reach their level on Instagram. Learning all of the tips in this book will enable you to surpass them.

"If you really look closely, most overnight successes took a long time."

— Steve Jobs

Chapter 3

Optimize Your Account

Stand Out From The Crowd

Did you have fun spying on your competitors? You probably didn't even know that you had so many competitors. It may seem discouraging knowing that there are so many competitors who are already seeing results on Instagram and you are just starting. Shit, it may even feel like it is too late for you even to start. This is why it is vital to understand *how your company is different and why customers should be coming to you and not going to your competitors.* If you are not aware why your business is better, you are in a lot of trouble, my friend!

Before we move forward, I want you to go ahead and write down how your business is different from your competitors. This is going to be a part of your business message.

_____

_____

_____

_____

_____

_____.

We are going to focus on keeping your business message consistent throughout your Instagram account as we start optimizing it. This chapter is exciting because it is the first chapter where you will begin building your business on Instagram the correct way.

As we start optimizing your account, you will notice that I view an Instagram account as a business website. Your website needs to have your business message, call to actions, credibility, and it needs to be user-friendly. If your website is not optimized correctly, no matter how much traffic you drive to it, it will not convert. This is why I want us to take the time right now to set up your Instagram account correctly before we start driving traffic to it.

Bio

We will start with your bio. I consider the bio as the top portion of your home page when someone visits your website. What is the first thing a visitor sees when they go to your website? Well, I can tell you what they should see. Prior to them scrolling, they should be able to see the business name, business message, and a call to action. Your Instagram bio needs to consist of the same elements, plus a line of credibility.

To start with optimizing your bio, take a look at your Instagram username and name. Your username should be your business name, but the name section should be more involved. I like using the name portion to include more titles. Instagram users search for specific keywords, like *photographer,* and users that have the word *photographer* in the name will show up on the search result. In addition to adding a title to your name, adding a location is just as powerful. If you were a photographer, for example, you could set up your name to say something such as, "Tampa's Top Photographer."

The next step is adding your business message in the bio. Having your business message in the bio is VERY important! The business message is the top influencer in converting your followers. There are numerous accounts on Instagram offering the same services or products that you are. This is where you are going to differentiate yourself and target your specific audience. When a user lands on your account, your business message needs to speak to them.

Tell them who you are targeting, how you can help them, and what tools you are going to use to help them. Using the photographer as an example again, the photographer can say, "Helping Entrepreneurs Look More Professional With The Perfect Portrait Shoot." I hope you noticed how the whole business message must fit in less than nine words. You are only allowed 150 characters in your bio, and you still need to include your credibility and call to action. You may need to play around with the wording, but do not leave any of these steps out. If even one of these crucial steps is missing, your account will not convert.

The third element that you need to include in your bio is credibility. Again, many accounts are promising a variety of things on Instagram. Your business needs to position itself as a leader in the industry and to do this your business message must be definite, and you need to have a small source of credibility in the bio. The source of credibility does not have to be long, but you do need to include something for you to win your visitors' trust. This section can be an award that you won, the amount of money that you save your clients, or the number of clients that you have helped overall, etc.

The final optimization step for your bio is the *call to action*. Let us say that your potential client just visited your account; they read your business message, and they concluded that your company provides something that they need. Your bio also explained what services you would use to help them and you developed some initial trust with your visitor because they reviewed your source of credibility. Now you have to direct them to a call to action to convert them. Right under the credibility portion, you should implement a call to action. The call to action can say, "Click The Link Below For A Free Consultation" or "DM Me For Inquiries." As long as you have a direct call to action, your bio will be optimized to convert.

If you would like to see an example of an optimized Instagram account, you can take a look at my personal Instagram account (@amelkilic).

Please keep it clean and comfortable to view. Start every key point on its own line. I see way too many Instagram accounts that write everything out together. Remember, the harder it is for a customer to understand what you do and how they can become a customer, the less likely they will actually become one.

Keep It Simple

If you want me to prove the theory scientifically, I can do that! Humans naturally use calories for activities, we all know that. In a survival state, we choose to reserve our calories for serious actions. If an unnecessary task is burning many calories, humans walk away from it so that they can preserve it for more critical functions. Your visitors will only invest a limited amount of calories to understand what you are selling to them. Make sure that you only include vital information in your bio. I am sure that you believe that your service is essential and necessary, but if you do not keep your message simple, the potential customer will leave your account before they give your company a chance.

Now that you understand the importance of keeping a simplistic and intentional bio, I will give you an example of an account that **does not** have a call to action in the bio.

A potential client recently visited your Instagram account, and they noticed that you are a local restaurant. Your business name is at the top of the bio, and you stated that your restaurant has the best shrimp tacos in town. Great, they will take a look at your excellent images of the food and then leave your account. Why did they leave? Because you did not have a call to action in your bio. Believe it or not, people like to be told what to do. Being directed takes less effort than discovering directions. Please give them a reason why they should come to your restaurant!

Here is an example of an optimized bio. Your bio now has an optimized business name, your business message, credibility, and a call to action with a link associated with the call to action.

Tampa's Top Shrimp Tacos
Don't believe us?
Click the link for 20% off your first visit
www.tampashrimptaco.com

Profile Picture

Your profile picture does not play an immense role in the conversion process, but I nevertheless need to clear up a few points. If you are a business owner and have a business logo, use the logo as your profile picture. If people already associate the business logo to the company, then use it for Instagram as well. It is vital to keep the same tone across all of your social business accounts and your website. I notice business accounts on Instagram using images of their team or the owner. You may believe that it is a good tactic to build personability, but your profile picture is not the right place for that. You can include personable content in your feed and stories, but all of your social media platforms should have the same profile image. If a user jumps from one social media account to another, having the same profile image will confirm that it is the same business.

For freelancers and entrepreneurs that do not have a logo, use a professional image of yourself. Do not include a picture with other people or your dog. I get that you believe that it is cute, but it is not professional. Remember that our goal is to grow your business using Instagram. If you aspire to grow your following, you can create a different

Instagram account for your personal images. For your optimized account, keep it optimized.

Bio Link

If you optimized your business message and call to action accurately, your visitors should be clicking on the link in your bio. The next question is, where is the link leading them? If you promised a discount, the link better direct me straight to the discount. If it takes me to your business home page and I have to look for the discount, I will exit out of it within five seconds.

If you are ever unsure of what to do when it comes to optimizing and monetizing your Instagram account, always think of clean and simple. Trust me, if they want more information, they will find it. There is no need to shove everything down their throat right away. The only reason they clicked on your link is because they want the discount that you promised them. They do not care that you created the restaurant because your grandma's dog died and she used to cook for him all the time.

The link in the bio can lead your visitors to any website link on the internet. Choose your link wisely because Instagram does not allow you to attach links in many different channels. Remember to ask yourself what your business goal is with Instagram and if the link that you attached will help you achieve the goal. You can send your visitors to your business website, YouTube channel, or blog, for example.

Landing Page

What works best for our clients and our own business are landing pages. Unless your company sells products, I would highly advise directing your traffic to a landing page that is capable of capturing their contact information. Your objective should not be to close your visitors with the first link that you direct them to. The bounce rate on links directed from social media networks, especially Instagram, are really high and you will miss out on a lot of potential business. Landing pages work well because there is less room for error. If you send a visitor to your website, many different variables can turn off your potential client. With a landing page, if you built the trust through Instagram, they will not have any issues submitting their contact information.

Note that Instagram users spend very little time on a particular task, so you have about five seconds for them to see what you do (bio) and sign up for your service (bio link). If you are sending them to your home page where it would take more than three minutes to look over your business message and services, there is a high chance that they will just exit without signing up.

Keep the landing page simple. The landing page should be consistent with your bio. Include the business name and reiterate the same message you told your visitor before they clicked on the link. After that, include another small call to action and a form that they can submit to sign up for your service or a free consultation and wa-lah, you just got another new lead from Instagram. Sounds easy, right? Honestly, it is when you fully optimize your Instagram account. Instagram has been the top lead generator for our clients and for us, so we know that it works.

We love when we hop on a call with someone who submitted their free consultation form, and they ask us if our process works. We cherish telling them, "Well, that is how we got you on the phone, so it unquestionably works!"

Content Creation

Content and captions are going to be the selling factors on your Instagram account. You told them what you do, how you can help them, and how they can become a customer. The content is what proves all of that. The content will be the conversion determinant. It is hard to perfect content that converts. This is why I will make sure to give you the essentials so that your content starts converting your traffic.

First, I want to address all the business professionals consistently posting low-quality images of their dogs and cats. Please do us all a favor and make a different Instagram account just for your dog or cat. I can almost hear you saying, "Well, that is the audience that I want to attract and having personal content on the account is essential." Great job! You acquired your Instagram marketing strategy from a mid-aged cat-loving mother who calls herself an "Instagram Account Manager," but who has never converted a follower to a paying client on Instagram before.

Now that you have cleaned up your Instagram account and probably deleted 90% of your content, let us discuss the ratio between business and personal content. The ratio should be 70/30. 70% of your content should be business oriented and 30% can be personal and team-oriented.

Next, I want you to go on Google and search "Instagram themes." Take a look at a few theme examples and pick one that you would like to use for your Instagram account. Having a theme will make your account look professional and invested in. Having a clean theme is like having a clean and organized store. You do not want people walking into your store and seeing that everything is disorganized. Trust me, visitors respect clean and organized Instagram accounts. They will respect the time and effort that you are putting into your Instagram account.

Okay, you cleaned up your Instagram account, and you picked a theme you would like to use. Now you will start posting. You are probably still wondering what to post. Well, you took a look at your competitor's content and discovered what types of images work well for your industry. Use those examples when you start taking and posting your images. After you capture your shots, follow the theme that you picked. Following the theme will help you understand what style of picture you should post next.

Keep in mind that bright and clean shots work well on Instagram. I also highly recommend that you post high-quality images. Everyone is posting images taken on their phone with bad lighting and no focal point. I would recommend that you hire a professional photographer to take a few shots for you. Remember, if you do not have money to invest in a photographer, you can always find people who find value in what you have to offer in exchange for their service. That is the ultimate collaboration.

Captions

The images should grab your visitor's attention. The caption is what sells the image and the service that you provide. It is time that you start making the most out of your captions. Do not just throw in a few hashtags and words and call it a day. Take a look at the accounts of big influencers like Dan Lok and Gary Vee; their captions look like blogs.

I get it, it was hard to figure out what to post, and now you have to think of a caption. Sorry, but if you want to dominate your market on Instagram, you will have to optimize everything. Good news is that when you get the hang of it, you will be able to think of captions without any issues.

I think of the caption in three stages. The first stage is focused on tying the image to the caption. Mention something that is relevant to the image or what you were doing when the image was taken. The second stage is the action. Share some actions that you are currently involved in. This could be a new project that you are working on or a general activity that you are doing that day. The third stage is the call to action. This is where you will direct your visitors to an action. You can send them to your URL link or ask them to direct message you.

An example of the three stages is as followed:

"The coffee shop in Channelside has the best egg sandwich in Tampa."

—

Just stopped by to get a bite before my meeting today. A client is looking to generate more traffic using Google and Facebook Ads. Look forward to being able to set up his account today!

—

By the way, If you have been trying to set up Google ads for your business, I have a blog on the top strategies. The link is in my bio. Check it out and let me know if it helped.

—

Also, keep an eye on my story today. I will be giving away a free book to one of my followers!

I included two call to actions in the example above, but I hope you got the concept. You can follow these stages with every caption. Keep in mind that keeping your content in sync with each other will drastically increase your engagement and conversion.

Let me explain; there are images, captions, and stories on Instagram. Each of these should be in sync with each other and shifting people from one to the other, as I did in the example above, sending my followers to my story. You can also do this throughout a series of posts. The first post can be about you getting ready to partake in an action; the next one can be you doing the action, and the third can state the results from the action.

Keeping the same message across your different channels of content will help with building your business brand and trust. You will be developing a storyline through your content, and since people naturally connect with stories, they are more likely to relate to your business. After you build a relationship with a follower, they will consistently "check-in" with your business and monitor your progress. Just like friends check-in on their friends to see what they are up to, Instagram users do the same with businesses that they have developed a relationship with.

"The way to get started is to quit talking and begin doing."

– Walt Disney

Chapter 4

Find Your Potential Clients

Identify Your Target Audience

Do you know who your target audience is? Every business needs to know who they are selling to. Just as critical, it is to know your Instagram goal; you need to know who your target audience is. To be clear, your target audience is your potential clientele. This chapter is the reason our Instagram monetizing and growth strategy is different from all the other companies and from freelancers claiming that they will help you grow your Instagram account. Our focus is not to grow your Instagram; our goal is to grow your business using Instagram. Our goal is to help you optimize your account and drive your potential clients to your account, where they will convert into paying clients.

In this chapter, we will crush any misbeliefs if you still think that your customers are not on Instagram. With almost a billion users on Instagram, your potential clients are on Instagram! The problem is that you do not know how to locate them. Lucky for you, I will give you all of our strategies to find and target your clients. In this chapter, we will cover how to find your potential clients, and in the next chapter, we will discuss how to target them.

Instagram, unknowingly, offers many different channels to find and target specific groups or audiences. I will give you the top three channels that have helped us grow our own and our clients' businesses.

When you started your company, you probably had a good idea who your potential clients were. You knew what age they were, their hobbies, and their location. For this step, think of your potential clients as hashtags, usernames, and geotags.

If you already have customers, I want you to find them on Instagram. After you find them, you will focus on their usernames, hashtags, and geotags. Let me break it down for you a little more.

Find all of your current customers and write down their usernames. When we start targeting your potential clients, we will go back to their account and target their followers. The idea here is if they are interested in your product or service, it is highly plausible that their followers have the same interests. Makes sense, right?

Targeting your current or past customer's followers is a great strategy, but I have an even better one. We can target your competitor's followers! Find your competitors on Instagram and write down their usernames. Your competitor's followers will be more targeted for your business. There is an even higher chance that the followers following your competitors like or use the service or product that they offer, which in essence is the service or product that you offer.

Hashtags

The next step is to take a look at the hashtags that your customers or competitors are using. As I said, if your customers are using specific hashtags, there is a high chance that other users using the same hashtags would have the same interests. Before you go ahead and start looking into hashtags, I want to discuss what many businesses and marketers do wrong.

If you were a realtor and I asked you to find your potential clients using hashtags, what hashtags would you look up? It would likely be #tamparealestate, #tamparealtor, or #homeforsaletampa. What is the problem with those hashtags? They are going to send you to the wrong accounts! I want you to take a step back and think about who would be using those hashtags. It would be other realtors! You do not want realtors; you want buyers and sellers. So think of the hashtags that your potential clients would be using. A few examples would be #movingtotampa #househuntingtampa #lovetampa. Start thinking outside of the box.

Now, you may have noticed that I used Tampa in the hashtag. This is because if you are a realtor in Tampa, you would want potential clients in Tampa. If I just searched up #househunting, that would give me users from all around the world; we want targeted users. After you understand what hashtags your potential clients would be using, search up the hashtag on Instagram. Instagram will display everyone who has used the hashtag previously. All you have to do now is go down the list, one by one, and connect with them.

Getting the list of potential clients under a hashtag is like having a room full of potential clients. You have them all in one place. Now you can start targeting them and try selling to them.

The final targeting option that we will cover is geotagging. If you do not know what geotags are, it is the location that users tag on their posts. You can find the geotag right above their image.

The great thing about Instagram is that it also allows you to search for posts under a specific location. How is this beneficial? Well, let me give you another secret. Just as I asked you to think about the specific hashtags that your potential clients would be using, I want you to think about the locations that they usually go to. Let's use the ice cream shop as an example again. Say you had an ice cream shop and you were looking for another way to find your potential clients on Instagram. You can search up the location of your competitors on Instagram, and you will be able to find all the customers that have tagged their posts in that specific location.

We just covered the top three ways to find your potential clients on Instagram. I want you to go ahead and answer the following questions below.

What hashtags are your customers/competitors using?

_____

_____

_____

_____.

What geotags are your customers/competitors using?

_____

_____

_____

_____.

What are your competitors/customers usernames?

_____

_____

_____

_____.

I hope you guys see how powerful this information is. You are walking into a room full of potential clients with these three targeting options. It does not get easier than this.

"There are no secrets to success. It is the result of preparation, hard work, and learning from failure."

– Walt Disney

Chapter 5

Target Your Potential Clients

Put Them In Your Crosshairs!

In this chapter, you will start selling and driving traffic and awareness to your business. This is where we begin targeting your audience and begin sending them through the Instagram funnel that you have created. This is where we start converting followers into paying customers. I am very excited to share all the tips I have for you guys! Instagram has just made it way too easy to find your potential clients and target them.

In the previous chapter, we discussed the three strategies you can implement to find your potential clients. I hope you took the time to fill out the questions in the previous chapter, because in this chapter we will look up your potential clients and start targeting them.

Before we jump in, I want you to understand that Instagram is a numbers game. You need to grab your potential client's attention. To do that, you will have to be in their face—a lot! Merely liking their posts will not give you the results that you need. The way I look at growing your business using Instagram is like dating in middle school. If you really like someone and you wanted to go out with them, or in business terms "close them," there are a few steps you would take before you ask them the big question. The steps to growing your business and closing potential clients using Instagram will be identical.

You would first stalk them, which means you would find them on Instagram using the strategies that we covered in the prior chapter. The next step is to let them know that you exist and that you desire their attention. The problem is that you are shy; so what would you usually do? You would follow them and start liking a few of their posts.

That is a great start! A little tip that I have for you is to like four to seven posts in a row, so when they look at their notifications, your name will come up consecutively a few times, and it will stand out. Remember that we are trying to grab their attention and build their trust. If you grasped their attention with only the first step and they end up checking out your Instagram account, and they liked what they saw, you might be able to close them immediately. For others, it may take more effort.

The next step is to leave genuine comments on their posts. No one likes generic comments, especially since there are so many accounts using bots, leaving comments that are not even in context with the image. Mention something about their image and try to direct them to your account or website. You can say, "Love the striped shirt! We just released a lot of similar designs. If you like them, I can give you a 20% discount." Connect with them and have a call to action in the comment.

The final approach is to send them a direct message. I mentioned that this is a numbers game and you are seeking to grab their attention. Instagram allows you to like, comment, and direct message users. Consider which one of those actions has the lowest amount of actions directed to a particular user. Most accounts receive over 200 likes per post and 10-30 comments. It is difficult to stand out and get their attention by just liking and commenting. Fortunately, most users only get approximately 2-3 new direct messages a day. If you want to play the numbers game and get their attention, you have the highest chance of being noticed by sending them a direct message.

Now, you may ask, why can I not just send a direct message to them from the beginning instead of liking and commenting first. The explanation is that you need to build some trust before sending them the direct message and trying to close them. Think of the direct message as the final selling point. It is the final approach; if you do not do it correctly, you will lose the sale.

I advocate sending them a direct message as soon as you get any engagement back from them. This can be them following you back, liking your posts, or even them just responding to the comment that you left on their post. If they engage back with you, there is a high chance that they went on your profile and saw what your business has to offer.

Do not try to close them in your first direct message. You are still trying to build trust. Get a feel for any issues that they have in which you believe your business can resolve. Approach them with a solution and ask what it would take for them to move forward with your services. This step is solely about sales. If you are not a good salesperson, I highly advise for you to look into SPIN selling.

If you follow these steps, you will consistently drive traffic and awareness to your Instagram account. As I mentioned earlier, several users will visit your account after your first action; if your account is optimized correctly, you will be able to close them immediately. The process would partake in this sequence: You grab your potential clients' attention through our engagement techniques; they visit your Instagram account and notice that you offer something they need help with. Upon viewing your bio, they would scroll down to your content to verify your credibility. Then they follow your call to actions that you have implemented throughout your account; they click on your website link and visit your landing page. Finally, they sign up and become a client. It sounds pretty simple, and it is when everything is implemented as we discussed so far in the book.

Setting Up Your Instagram Shoppable

The sale process gets even simpler if you are operating an e-commerce. Instagram's shoppable posts feature made it easier than ever for businesses to sell their products on a social media platform. Prior to the feature being released, the only way to unite your followers with your products was through links. The shoppable feature creates a seamless experience for your followers to purchase your products right from your Instagram posts.

To create a shoppable Instagram account, you will need to connect your Instagram business profile to a Facebook catalog. If you do not have a Facebook catalog, you will need to create one under the business manager account that owns the Facebook page linked to your Instagram business account. If you are using Shopify, the process of transferring your products to the Facebook catalog is a lot easier than doing it manually.

Upon transferring your products to the Facebook catalog, your Instagram account will be automatically reviewed. After all of this is completed, tagging your products to your posts is very simple. When you get ready to post your image, tap the Tag Products icon and select the product from your catalog.

When your followers see your shoppable post, they will notice that the post is marked with a shopping bag icon. After you create your shoppable posts, notify your followers through your stories that you have made it easier for them to shop your products directly from your posts. It is a great way to spread the word and drive more traffic to your posts.

"If you really want to do something, you'll find a way. If you don't, you'll find an excuse."

– Jim Rohn

Chapter 6
Beat The Algorithm

Target Your Content

"Instagram changed their algorithm, and now I do not get as much engagement on my posts!" How many times did you hear someone complain about that before—or maybe you are one of them? The reason you are not getting much engagement anymore is that your content sucks, period. It is not Instagram's fault; it is your fault. All Instagram did was prioritize content that gets a high volume of engagement.

Instagram's algorithm is optimized to reward content that is good. How do they distinguish what is good? Well, by the engagement. Content that gets a lot of engagement is considered good because what Instagram believes is that if people are engaging with a particular post, they must like it.

They want people to stay on their app, so their theory is if they promote engaging content, visitors are likely to spend more time on the app.

So how do you beat the algorithm? You have to get a lot of engagement, and you have to get it fast. As soon as you post to your feed, users must start engaging with your content either through likes or comments. This is why hashtags are incredibly advantageous. Many accounts target hashtags, so when you post content with hashtags, you will get higher visibility and engagement on your posts. Also, make sure to respond to the comments as soon as possible because that will boost up your number of comments on your post. It all counts!

This is why I mentioned earlier to post engaging captions. Ask a question in your caption or direct them to engage with your post. If you are a member of any group chats, share your posts there and ask the group members to leave some love on your posts.

However, it does not just end there. Instagram wants to know that people are engaging with your entire account, not just your posts. Instagram also considers the number of views, shares, saves, swipe ups, and DM's that your account is getting overall. Views can come from video posts, stories, and even your highlights. What matters most is that your followers and customers are overall engaging with your business account on Instagram.

Let's jump into some hacks that you can implement that will generate more account engagement.

Highlights

Do you have any story highlights? Story highlights are a great way to start engaging your current followers. If you do not know what a story highlight is, let me explain real quick. You already know what stories are; well, you can actually save them under a category or "highlight" on your profile and they will stay there until you decide to take them off. Highlights are a great way to show off your products, services, customers, team, and demos.

After you create your Instagram story highlights, you will need to start implementing call to actions that will drive your followers to the highlights. You can set up the call to actions in your new story posts or in your captions. An example of a call to action in the caption can be a picture of a dish that you made and directing your followers to your highlight to see the cooking instructions. Another example can be a post of a new service that your company will start providing; you can direct them to your highlight by saying, "View the full demo in our highlight."

This strategy can be followed for every industry. You can create highlights of different blog posts, downloads, workouts, or travel guides, for example.

Scheduling Posts

The next step to increasing your overall account engagement is to start scheduling your feed posts so that you can focus on making more stories and begin engaging with your followers. Scheduling Instagram posts can save you hours of work. It is hard to sit down every day and figure out what to post and what to write in the captions. By the time you do that, you probably do not even make the time for the stories or to engage with other users on Instagram. This is why it is best to dedicate an hour every week to plan out all of your posts for the week.

There are plenty of free apps that will allow you to schedule your Instagram posts, simply google "free Instagram post scheduler." Instagram did announce that they may create an in-app scheduler, so that will make it easier than ever to schedule your posts.

Another benefit of scheduling your posts is that you will be able to schedule the posts at the time that your followers are most engaged on Instagram. As mentioned earlier, you will want engagement on your posts as fast as possible; this is why it is important to post your content during high-engaging times. To find the best time to post, take a look at your insights.

Stories

Since Instagram is driving more traffic to stories, it is essential to make sure you consistently have content in your story. The good news is that stories do not have to be as high quality as your feed posts. Instagram stories are becoming the biggest thing in the social media world, yet only a few businesses are taking advantage of it. This is your opportunity to get ahead of the game.

People are creatures of habit and they like watching the same people on their stories day after day. If you can grab their attention, you will always have loyal and curious followers. By posting to your stories consistently, you are training your followers to expect content from you.

Instagram is consistently releasing new Instagram story features that allow you to engage with your followers. A few of those features are polls, countdown timer, question box, and more. Your job is to use these features to get your followers to engage with your story. Another huge feature is the swipe up feature if you have over 10,000 followers.

Instagram is keeping track of all the engagement that your account is receiving, so rack up your points and make your way to the top of the algorithm!

Those are all various ways to increase your accounts engagement, but do not forget to engage with your followers as well. Your followers are like friends. For them to stay loyal, they will require some attention from you as well. We all have friends that require more attention than others; give them what they require to keep them as an engaged follower.

"Some people dream of success while others wake up and work hard at it."

– Winston Churchill

Chapter 7
Become Consistent

Implement Your Strategies

By this stage, you have completed a majority of the hard work and your Instagram account will be optimized to convert. After you optimize your Instagram account, you do not have to edit it again. The only time you will edit the initial stages is if your account is not converting. Like an ad or email campaign, you may have to AB test a few different variables until you discover what strategy will work best for your business and message. Upon discovering the right variables for your Instagram account, and when you begin converting your follower to paying clients, I want you to 10x the traffic to your account. When you have something that genuinely works, squeeze the hell out of it. If your Instagram is converting, this is your opportunity to scale your business at rates you were never able to do so previously.

As you already know, I view an Instagram account as a website. Everything that you have optimized in the previous chapters is similar to setting up funnels for your website. Every channel and post on Instagram is a funnel that directs your followers to a call to action. After the funnel is optimized, your sole job is to drive traffic to your account. Your account is worthless unless you are consistently driving traffic to it, which take me to this chapter's motive—consistency.

I will assume that you are a business owner if you are reading this book. If you are, I don't have to explain the importance of continuously working hard and expanding your knowledge to create a successful business. You knew that it was critical to have a clear path and to put in a lot of work to get to where you are today. Many sleepless nights and missed events were invested in your business. If you want to take your business to the next level, these are your next steps. This is where I need you to get back in the driver's seat and start driving your business to the next level.

When you complete this book and do not see any results in two months, ask yourself if you have implemented every step in the book and if you were consistent. Don't criticize the tips in the book if you don't see results, because they have worked for over 2,000 accounts so far. Take the time now and tell yourself that you will do what it takes to become a leader in your industry on Instagram and start generating sales using the platform.

This chapter is centered on your mindset. I will give you all of the tools that you need, but it is up to you to implement them and become consistent. I always find it amazing how many people that attend my class never end up implementing any of the strategies. Two or three months later, they are still in the same place, wondering how to grow their business using Instagram. There are two types of characters in this world, be the one that people look up to and wish they were, be a leader in your industry!

Majority of people have a desire to be successful. Sadly, only a few know what it takes to become successful. This is the reason why so many businesses fail. It is not that the business was a bad idea, but rather the fact that the founder had a vision of overnight success. The belief of overnight success makes people shortcut-minded and impatient.

In reality, overnight success does not exist. Statistically, you are more likely to succeed by playing the lottery. Overnight success is merely the market realizing the value of a great product, which could have been in the shadow of its competitors for a long time.

If entrepreneurship was easy, wouldn't every lucid person pursue it? Unfortunately, they are pursuing it! There are way too many wantrepreneurs believing if Instagram, Snapchat, Facebook, Uber, and Airbnb founders were able to build multibillion-dollar companies in several years, so can they. What most people do not realize is that they are selecting the outliers as a benchmark and they are underestimating the resources invested in these companies for them to be able to reach such levels of success. This is the awakening phase of your career.

In the awakening phase, potential entrepreneurs realize that the journey is not as linear as they presumed. Self-awareness and inner motivation are your long-term drivers. When you know exactly what everything is tied to, you know why things are happening and where they will be many years in the future. I want you to ask yourself how every decision you make from now on will impact you in three years. The biggest problem our generation faces is that we are only able to create short-term goals.

It was after my second startup that I realized what my motive was. My greatest motivation in life is the difference that I can make. It is the difference that I can make for other business owners and entrepreneurs looking to scale in business and life. I am fully committed to entrepreneurship because it allows me to create a more significant difference in the world.

Why did you choose entrepreneurship? Find the real reasons and motives today; they will drive your 10-year overnight success.

"Many of life's failures are people who did not realize how close they were to success when they gave up."

– Thomas Edison

Chapter 8
Hire Influencers

Influence Your Target Market

You have probably heard of Instagram influencers, and if you have not, I recommend researching more about them. Instagram influencers are Instagram users who have established credibility and an audience, who can persuade others by their trustworthiness and authenticity. Brands use influencers to reach out to the influencer's audience. If done right, the ROI of hiring influencers can be ridiculous. There are just several indispensable key pointers that we will go over before you go and find someone and pay them a whole bunch of money without any return.

Finding the right influencer can be difficult. The first pointer is making sure the influencer suits your brand story. Ask yourself if your business and the influencer are a good match. Do not merely look at their following and consider that they are the right influencer for your brand. I understand that you may believe that if an influencer has a big following, there must be someone that will be interested in your product or service. This may be true to a particular degree, but think about the image that the influencer is projecting, because that is the crowd that they are drawing.

Let me give you an example. Say you are a luxury watch company and you were looking to grow your awareness through influencers. You would probably tell yourself that everyone needs a watch, so as long as you can reach a big audience, you will get someone who is interested in buying a watch. Again, it is accurate to a certain degree, but say you hired an influencer whose brand is focused on local food, or let's even say you find an influencer whose focus is around watches, but most of the brands that the influencer has on their account are inexpensive watch companies. His followers would be primed to that specific group. If all of a sudden they post an expensive watch, not only does it not fit their theme, but the post will reach the wrong people. It will reach people who are used to paying up to $70 for a watch, not $350.

Let's think outside of the box again. What influencers or brands would have the same target audience as you? It would be a business-oriented account or one that is focused on high-end outfits. These accounts would have the followers that would be interested in your product. If you discover a business brand oriented around business outfits or lifestyle, they are more than likely to have followers of high influence and ones who have the money to pay for your high-end watch. The next step is to decide which influencers have a good engagement on their account.

You will notice accounts that have many followers but their engagement is low. How can this be? Well, they either do not engage with their audience and their content is not engaging, or their followers are fake. Find an Instagram account engagement calculator on Google and type in their username. The engagement percent should be above 4%.

After you discover around twenty relevant accounts that fit your brand story and have a good engagement percentage, you can begin contacting them. When you start contacting them, you will run into the second key point that you should be aware of. What are they asking for in exchange for promoting your brand on their page? You will discover many different responses, making it difficult to decide which influencer is worth the investment.

Ask the influencer for the analytics of their previous promotions that they did for other brands. You can track how many username sticker tabs or swipe ups there were on a story post. Unfortunately, you cannot track the username tabs in the caption yet, but you can ask for the insights on their posts and see how many impressions they get. Even though they can't track tags in their caption, they could direct the traffic from the caption to their URL link, which is trackable in two ways. You can create a bit.ly link, or they will be able to see the number of URL link clicks on their account analytics. If they are not converting any followers, do not waste your time and money with them. Even though an influencer can receive over a thousand likes on their post, it does not mean that they can convert their followers to real traffic for a business. It all depends on their relationship with their followers.

When it comes to pricing, you, as a business owner, will have to decide what is a reasonable ROI. If you are selling watches that cost $140 and the influencer is asking for $100 per post, ask yourself if you will be able to sell at least one watch to make your investment back. Using influencers is tricky, but when used correctly, they are powerful.

"Always deliver more than expected."

– Larry Page

Chapter 9

Implement Call to Actions

Seek Action

If you take anything from this book, take this—you need strong call to actions! The reason this chapter is critical is that the majority of your competitors are not utilizing call to actions and this step will be your opportunity to crush them in the Instagram game. Also, without them your Instagram traffic will not convert because you never told them how to convert. Sounds dumb, right? However, it is true. If you implemented all the strategies that we covered so far, you would develop a big following, but the following will only help you develop a brand. Our goal is not to grow our followers, but to convert them into paying customers, which will grow our business.

We already discussed the implementation of call to actions throughout the book, but I felt that I needed to break it down even more. There are four different techniques to drive an action on Instagram. To start, pick two out of the four techniques and start utilizing them on your Instagram account. As you advance with your Instagram strategy, implement the other two techniques afterward. The reason I want you to start with only two CTAs initially is due to your current followers. The call to actions will request an action from your followers. If you implement all four from the start, your followers will start feeling pressured and are highly likely to *unfollow* you.

The first call to action that we will set up is in the bio. We optimized your bio earlier in the book, and if you followed the steps, your bio's call to action would already be in place. If you skipped over the steps, this is your opportunity to optimize it now. Since your bio will have your business message and credibility, it is essential to inform your visitors about how to receive the services that you promised them. The call to action can be as simple as, "Click the link below for a free consultation" or "Claim your coupon today." When a visitor lands on your Instagram account and reads your bio, the bio needs to be able to convert them. What is the point of driving traffic to your account if you are not optimized to convert them?

The second call to action will be in your caption. It is excellent that you are engaging your audience and including hashtags in your posts, but are you converting the users that see your content? If you follow the three stages of content creation that we discussed in the third strategy tip, your captions should contain a call to action. If you are providing value in your caption and giving your followers tips, you can always include a call to action below that. A few examples could be "Check out our most recent blog for all of the tips," or "Click on the link in my bio to get started and set up your free consultation."

By now, we already have two excellent call to actions. The third one will be in your stories. Just as you implemented call to actions in your captions, your next step will be to start implementing call to actions in your stories and live videos. There are three different actions that you can implement in your stories that can drive an action. The three actions are statements during live videos, text in the story, or the swipe-up feature.

The swipe-up feature is a feature that is granted for users that have over 10,000 followers. Everyone's initial goal with Instagram is to reach 10,000 followers because we all know how powerful this feature is. The swipe-up feature allows you to attach a link to your story, which your viewer can easily access by simply swiping up. If you have the swipe-up feature, do not misuse it during the early stages. As we all know, humans are creatures of habit. Your initial intention with the swipe-up feature is to get your viewers used to swiping up on your stories. The strategy in developing this habit is by consistently providing high amounts of value for free. For the next few months, your story strategy should be to provide links to tips, strategies, and data that is relevant to your following. After you build their trust and develop a relationship emerged around value, only then should you send them to a link intended to convert your viewer.

If you do not have over 10,000 followers, don't worry! The other two actions that you can implement in your stories are just as powerful. Instagram stories allow you to insert a question box in your story. The question box is a lead generator.

An example of how to utilize it can be if you posted a screenshot of your ebook and placed the question box with a statement saying, "Submit your email to receive a free copy of the ebook." We just converted a question box into a lead gen form! If you do not want to include the question box, your second option would be to place a text in your story with the same call to action. Your viewers can submit their information by directly replying to the story.

The third action for your story is very similar to the previous one. This action will be implemented during live videos. If you are not utilizing live videos yet, you should! Live videos receive a high engagement because it is raw and followers enjoy connecting with you during live sessions where they can ask you questions and engage with you instantly. During a live video, you can direct your viewers to different channels on your Instagram account. If you are discussing a case study in the live video, you can direct your viewers to your URL in the bio to sign up for a free consultation.

I hope you are aware that Instagram's primary focus for the next few years is to direct their users to the stories. This is why it is vital that you do not skip this step. Posting stories with an intentional call to action is just as important as your feed post. Make sure your call to actions are in sync with each other. If you are directing your visitors all over the place, they will get confused and you will lose their trust.

Keep it consistent throughout your account. All of your call to actions should be focused on your business objective or Instagram goal.

The final call to action—and the most powerful one—will be in your direct message. Do you know why the CTA in the DM is the most powerful? I would love to explain! It is simply because the direct message is personal and "direct." Direct calls to action perpetually work better than general ones. When you directly approach someone and ask them to do a task, they are more likely to do it than if you ask a group of people to do an action.

The direct message is also the only other place that you can attach a link on Instagram other than the URL in your bio—unless you have over 10,000 followers; if so, you can then include it in the story as well. The direct messages will take up the most of your time but they will also have the highest ROI, so it is worth your investment. Keep in mind that Instagram has a quick reply option; you can simply set up a generic message and send it to all of your potential clients.

We just covered one of the most critical chapters in the book. If you need to go back and verify your call to actions, this is your opportunity to do it. It is vital that you understand the importance of call to actions and how to implement them on your Instagram account.

Below I will include seven additional copyright and strategy tips for your call to actions.

1. Enforce users to take action

Our goal with our post is not to just share but also for our users to take action. Use action words such as *shop now, click below,* and *call now.*

2. Sell

We are in business to sell. Don't worry about being too *salesy.* If you present yourself as a business, they will expect to be sold to; grant them what they desire after you build your value.

3. Create an urgency

Call us today works better than *call us.* People react to limited time, and they are more likely to react to your call to action. When people sense a lot of action, they want to be part of it. Make it seem like a lot of people are interested in your product or service.

4. It's all about the reader

Write in the reader's perspective. People only care about themselves. Point out their pain points in their perspective. Take the "so...?" test after you write your copy. If you can respond to the copy with "so...?" it is not good enough.

5. Images speak a thousand words

Include your product, service, or business message in the image.

6. Stick with your business tone

If you are sending users to different links, make sure the process is as clear and straightforward as possible. Even the smallest difference in tone can cause the visitor to lose trust.

7. Put some muscle in your call to action

Make sure your call to action stands out. Do not cram it in with the rest of the copy. Put some weight on it.

"What do you need to start a business? Three simple things: know your product better than anyone, know your customer, and have a burning desire to succeed."

– Dave Thomas

Chapter 10

Become a Brand

Know Your Why, How And What

I finally have a fun chapter for you! Did you develop a brand behind your business, or is it just a company? In this chapter, we will provoke your creativity and urge you to learn about yourself and your company.

Even though I stated that it would be a fun chapter, it will also be a difficult one. Branding is not an easy task, but it is an essential one. Why? Because you need to stand out. Unless you have a very unique business and do not have any competitors—which is doubtful—you will have to find a way to differ from them. I want you to ask yourself how you are different. We covered this at the beginning of the book when we discovered your business message. This is your opportunity to tweak what you wrote earlier and create a killer business message. We will break down your business brand around three questions. The questions are why, how and what. What most companies do wrong is they answer their questions in the sequence of what, how, why, but what sets big companies apart, such as Apple, is that they start with their why.

Why?

The why is the core reasons that you started the company. Why did you even start the company that you currently have? What was the motive? To save you trouble in the future, your why should not be to make money. Companies that chase money habitually never last, because a lot of hard work is invested into a company before they start seeing results, so people who are chasing money quit before they can even grow a business big enough to start generating revenue.

I recommend focusing your why around your marketing and your clientele. People use companies in which they share the same values. Most consumers do not buy what you do, but instead, why you do it. I also recommend that you implement this approach in everything that you do in life. Starting with the why will build the value from the beginning, and it will be much easier to close your potential client after you explained your why. People are tired of just being sold to; they want to give their time and money to people with whom they share the same values.

How? What?

The how is the way you plan on fulfilling your why. Many believe that the how is the final product, but it is not. The how is the process that you will take to create the what. How do you plan on fulfilling your motive? After you figure out your why and how, the what is easy, because it is the final product of your motive.

I will give you Apples why, how and what as an example.

Why: Everything we do, we believe in challenging the status quo. We believe in thinking differently.

How: The way we challenge the status quo is by making our products beautifully designed, simple to use, and user-friendly.

What: We happen to make great computers.

After you understand your why, how, and what, it is important to start pushing your message through the content that you produce on Instagram. These steps are crucial, not just for Instagram, but for your business in general. The approach should also be used for your business message on your website, emails, and business meetings.

If you think you got it right, go to your Instagram account with the mindset of a new visitor and ask yourself if you can figure out what the company does, who their target audience is, and how are they different from their competitors. You can always ask a friend or a stranger to answer those questions if you are too biased to do it yourself.

A successful Instagram brand has a consistent, clear message and tone throughout its account. This includes their bio, theme, stories, feed posts, captions, influencers, and hashtags. Your job as a successful business owner or marketer is to tie everything that we covered in this book and implement the strategy for your business or client and create a successful Instagram marketing campaign.

Remember that people connect to brands and messages, not to products and services. Do not ever stop building your brand!

"If people like you, they'll listen to you, but if they trust you, they'll do business with you."

– Zig Ziglar

Chapter 11

Instagram Ads

Promote Your Business

Everything that we covered in the book so far can be done for free. This chapter requires a financial investment, but do keep in mind that every business needs to have a marketing budget. If you are not reinvesting in your brand or business, you are slowing down or maybe even reversing your growth.

As humans, we are limited to the number of actions that we are capable of completing at any given moment. Do not hold the growth of your business in your hands alone. One of the biggest mistakes that novice business owners make is that they do not implement outside resources to help them grow their business. Trust me; I understand that you have been dedicating a lot of effort to your business and you presumably just started generating positive cash flow. However, the worst mistake that you can make right now is to spend the money on activities that will not support your business growth. Reinvesting in your business is crucial in the first few years. Reinvesting can be hiring employees, implementing marketing services, or even creating ads.

We are going to take the time now to incorporate ad strategies that you can implement and start generating more awareness, leads, and sales for your business. If you have not created ads before—and I am not referring to promoting your Instagram posts—I want you to familiarize yourself with the ad manager platform. The reason I recommend using the ad manager over simply promoting your posts on Instagram is that you have more targeting and optimization options. Promoting your content through the Instagram app is excellent for awareness but not for conversion-focused objectives.

Keep in mind that you can edit your ad placements in the ad manager if you want the ads to show on Instagram and not on Facebook. Why you have to use the Facebook ad manager? Because Facebook owns Instagram and they have one ad manager for both platforms.

Setting up ads is tough, especially setting up ads that convert. Numerous variables can impact your conversion. There are various styles of ads, such as an informative approach, emotional, or even lifestyle. Knowing what strategy to use will greatly depend on your industry and your ad objective.

Setting Up Instagram Ads That Convert

With over a million advertisers currently promoting on Instagram, it is getting tougher and tougher to convert users through ads. Everyone is competing for user attention. Fortunately, Instagram ads still yield a high number of engagement and conversions compared to other advertising platforms. Let's dive into a few ad techniques that you can start implementing today that will help you grow your business.

For the first ad technique that I have for you, I want you to refer to your business message. We already created your business message at the beginning of the book, and you stated how your business is capable of resolving a problem that your clients have. Include your customer's pain points in the ad. Nothing grabs someone's attention more than pain.

Every product or service is built for a cause, and the cause revolves around pain points. If you have watched the movie, Wolf of Wall Street, I am sure you remember the pen scene. In order to sell the pen, he needed to create a pain point. It is not about the product working; it is about the reason the product works.

The next technique in creating ads that convert is to implement storylines in the ad. People love stories, especially when there is an emotional connection. Make sure your story has a beginning, middle, and end. The end is the problem that your service or product solves.

An example of a story is a group of women who have low confidence because of their bad skin and the skin products that they need are very expensive. The business marketing to them solves their problem by offering a product that resolves their skin issues for a manageable price. Since the women can afford the products, they start utilizing the products. The final result is a group of women with glowing skin and a ton of confidence. That is a story that appeals to pain points and emotions. There was a problem, a middle, and a resolution at the end. It is not about the product; it is about the problem that the product can resolve. Replicate this strategy for your business and utilize it in your ads.

The next Instagram ad technique is to start utilizing videos over images. Videos are booming on social media currently! You can use videos to show product tutorials or testimonials for example, but make sure that within the video you cover the pain points and how your product or service can resolve the problem.

To get the best results with video ads, include captions to every video ad that you run. The reason you should include the caption is that videos start playing as soon as a user scrolls down to it, but it does not play the audio until the user clicks on the video. The beginning of the video contains vital information; you do not want users missing the important introductory info.

When you get ready to start creating your ads, it is vital to AB test different variables on the ad. Before we move forward, I want to make sure that you still understand what AB testing is. AB testing ads is when you create the same ad twice and only change one variable, like the thumbnail for example, and then track the analytics to see which ad is converting better. When you find the ad that is converting better, you will stop the other one and create another AB test from the ad that is providing better results and change another variable until you AB tested every variable and discover the ad that offers the best results for your goal.

I understand that this can get pretty technical, but even if you develop a small understanding on creating ads, it can bring you plenty of growth. Keep in mind that more and more businesses are going to start using Facebook and Instagram ads, so your cost per result will end up going up. This is also why you should start implementing ads as soon as possible. It is still one of the most efficient and cost-effective sources of marketing out there compared to traditional marketing.

Another valuable tip when it comes to capturing leads using Facebook or Instagram ads is rather than sending users to your landing page, use the lead capture form within the ad itself. So rather than sending users to a different link, they can click on sign up on the ad and submit their information without having to leave the platform. The reason utilizing the form within the ad is more effective is that the action is consistent within the platform, which eliminates the chances of your landing page not fitting the same tone. People lose trust if they get redirected to a different link and the interface is different. It also helps with the loading time, since they do not have to wait for your website to load, which gives them the chance to exit out before they are given the opportunity to sign up.

Setting Up Retargeting Ads

Have you ever visited a website and then saw an ad on Facebook or Instagram selling you a product that you were just looking at? It feels creepy, but it is very effective. Retargeting, also known as remarketing, allows you to target users that visited your website and expressed an interest in your products or services. Only about 2% of web traffic converts on the first visit; this is why retargeting is vital in growing your business.

Retargeting is a cookie-based technology that allows you to follow your visitors anonymously. You will have to embed a Facebook pixel to your website. The pixel will send data back to the ad manager on which pages were viewed on your site by a particular visitor. You can even target visitors that added products to their cart but never completed their purchase.

To set up your retargeting ad, you will log in to your Facebook Ads manager and select audiences. Next, you will click on create audience and then custom audience.

You will have a few options displayed for your custom audience, but for retargeting, you will select website traffic.

On the next screen, you will be able to select different audiences that you would like to retarget. A few of the options are anyone who visits your website, people who visit specific pages, and people visiting specific web pages but not others. I recommend going with anyone who visits your website at the beginning. You can create different audiences as you start getting more technical with your targeting strategies.

If you've already create a pixel, great! If you haven't, the next step will be to create a pixel specific to your target audience and embedding it to your website. You can also download the Facebook pixel helper afterward. The Facebook pixel helper is a plugin on chrome that allows you to verify that your pixel is installed correctly on your website.

After you verify your Facebook pixel and create a custom audience, you are ready to create a retargeting ad utilizing one of the ad techniques that we discussed earlier.

Ads are an additive to your consistent Instagram engagement. Remember that our goal is to always be in our potential clients face with high quality and optimized content. The ads will follow them even after they visit your Instagram account and website.

"Your most unhappy customers are your greatest source of learning."

– Bill Gates

Epilogue

A Little Story That Will Change The Way You Operate Your Business

Put Your Energy Where The Profits Are

Allow me to tell you a short story. This story has been one of the most significant game changers in my life and business, and I want to share it with you! I have also found this story to be the reason why some businesses can scale to over a million dollars in revenue while other businesses struggle to make it over 40K annually.

Say you were getting paid $1,000 for every mile that you ran. If you run five miles in a day, you would generate $5,000 a day. It took you four hours to run the five miles because that is all the time you had to dedicate to it.

The problem here is that you did not just invest four hours into the run. You also had to go to the store to buy the food that would need to have enough energy to complete the run; you also had to prepare the food, then you had to wash the dishes. Do not forget that you also have to wash your clothes for the next day and go to the store and replace your running attire when it wears out.

Let's say that all of the extra stuff took about another five hours of your day. That means that you invested nine hours in the run, which you got $5,000.

Where am I going with this? Five hours of your day were put into actions that *do not provide direct results.* Direct results are actions that deliver results *directly*, like getting paid for running. Getting your clothes and food prepared are indirect actions.

The way you scale your business is by hiring or finding services that can do the indirect work for you. Examples of indirect actions in the business world can be content creation, product design, branding, customer service, or even cooking. Direct actions are sales, ads, or potential client meetings.

If you hired someone to do your shopping, cooking, and laundry, you might pay them around $1,000, but that means that you have those extra five hours to invest in your run, which would generate $5,000 in additional revenue. So at the end of the day, instead of generating only $5,000, now you are generating $9,000 after you pay the $1,000 to get your indirect work done.

That, my friends, is the secret to scaling your business.

About The Author

Amel Kilic is a serial entrepreneur, rebellious marketer, and a small business growth expert. He and his team have helped over hundreds of entrepreneurs and small businesses reach their business and life goals with a passion for helping businesses find new and innovative ways to leverage technology and marketing to facilitate rapid business growth.

Amel is curating his own brand of "NO BULLSHIT Business Growth" as he understands that a lot of business owners get tricked into paying "marketers" for unrealistic promises.

Want More Help, Or Looking To Set Up A Marketing Consultation? Go To: Gentechmarketing.com

Follow Amel Kilic on Instagram:

@amelkilic https://www.**instagram**.com/**amelkilic**

Printed in Great Britain
by Amazon